THE MILLENNIALS AND GEN Z BIBLE!

SELF-HEALTH FOR MILLENNIALS AND GEN ZS!

BY

NICK MULLER

A MODERN TAKE ON 200 MOTIVATIONAL QUOTES TO INSPIRE YOU TO BECAME THE BEST VERSION OF YOURSELF!

THE MILLENNIALS AND GENZ BIBLE

Right now, a vicious war is raging around the world. Even though every nation is involved, the mainstream media seems to ignore the undeniable evidence.

It is a different kind of war, but still, it is a war; instead of armies from different countries fighting to death against each other, we have two generations fighting. The Millennials against the GenZs are battling out with hashtags on social media to decide who is the cringest generation.

However, these two generations have more in common than the general public thinks. They each have gone through wars, different financial crises, and even a plague that shut down the whole world. These two generations are blessed and cursed to witness and experience the rise and development of technology, while still evolves as I write this.

Both generations, slightly obsessed with avocados, social media statues, and ice coffees, are the first generations ever where a person must be a millionaire to afford to buy a house.

That's why all the hate and discrimination against Millennials and GenZs is unfair. Yes, they have Netflix, Spotify, Tinder, and TikTok. However, previous generations could afford a house with minimum wages, had much better music and movies, and could get a date with someone hot because they were not even aware that hotter people existed.

Technology has been pushing the world to evolve faster than ever. Each new year brings a new gadget, a new cryptocurrency, and a new sexuality category. It's an ever-changing world, almost impossible to keep up with.

That is why, in this book, you will find a fresh interpretation for Millennials and GenZs of old motivational quotes, popular sayings, and mantras.

You will find wisdom in simple words and expressions, to navigate the hostile social media world, to recognize the sociopaths on dating ups, to be brave enough to go after your dreams, or just to finally get that face tattoo that you have been wanting forever.

So, turn off your social media notifications, put on your favorite playlist on Spotify, get your ice latte, spread that buttery avocado on your organic wholewheat toast, and let's have some fun.

1- "Don't take yourself so seriously; no one else does."

Seriously, nobody cares. Most people come from a generation that got participation trophies just for showing up in a competition. Some even have the audacity to display it proudly on a shelf in their living room.

Nowadays, moms everywhere shower their kids with compliments, and modern dads never miss a chance to express how proud they are. These overprotective behaviors create a fake illusion that, somehow, we are important and can't fail. That contributes to inertia and fear of trying.

The reality is that we are not that important; we are not special, and this is liberating. Most people are too busy trying not to ruin their own lives.

Stop overthinking. Ask that girl or the guy out. Speak up your opinion in the meeting. Buy the purple suit. Get that face tattoo that you always wanted.

2- "TRUE LOVE IS WHEN TWO PEOPLE LOWER THEIR STANDARDS JUST THE RIGHT AMOUNT."

Hollywood and the media have planted the idea of the perfect partner in our subconscious for years.

For women, they have the hot, muscular guy who is manly but very sensitive. The kind of man who likes to cuddle and talk about their dreams and childhood traumas after a rough sex session. For the men, they present you with skinny bimbo with big boobs that never complains about anything, loves sports, and sips semen like a cosmopolitan in happy hour.

These archetypes only exist in movies; there is nothing wrong with having standards, but not knowing when to lower your standards is a sure way to end up living alone in a small apartment, accompanied by half a dozen cats.

3- "DREAMS ARE THE FIRST THING PEOPLE ABANDON WHEN THEY UNDERSTAND HOW THE WORLD WORKS."

First, the Easter Bunny, then Santa, and when your world starts to slap your face with disappointments, bills, taxes, and lower back pain, you will abandon your dreams like someone abandoning their dignity after that fourth shot of tequila at 4 a.m.

A dream without a plan and a deadline is just a dream. If you are not born rich or have the looks of someone who won the DNA lottery, you will need to work hard to make your dreams become reality.

Even basic things like losing weight and being healthy are not easy for most of us normal human beings. We need to find the strength to go above and beyond, to go the extra mile, and if we want to have an extraordinary life, we need to be willing to do extraordinary things.

This is part of the process; you will have to become obsessed with your goals and dreams, and you will have to give 110% percent. You are giving birth to a new you, to your new life. It will be painful; there will be blood, sweat, and tears, but once you cross that finish line, it will be worth it.

4- "BE THE PIECE OF SHIT YOU WANT TO BE, NOT THE PIECE OF SHIT EVERYONE THINKS YOU ARE."

At the end of the day, we all suck. People suck. Otherwise, why would we have things like locks, guns, and restraining orders?

So, why would you spend your whole life trying to fulfill others' expectations of who you are?

It doesn't matter how nice you are; people will find something in you to complain about. They will think you are an asshole. So, own it. Embrace your uniqueness and be your own kind of asshole.

5-"You can't act like used "Adidas" and expect to be treated like "Louboutin."

D on't expect respect from other people if you don't respect yourself.

Draw lines, demand boundaries, let people know better than to fuck with you.

Be brutal about your dignity because once someone lose respect for you, they will never look at you the same way.

Don't be someone else's plan B or second-best option, and definitely never accept being someone's 3 am booty call.

6-"Being Who You Are, Pisses Off All the Right People."

Most people are by your side as longs you are at same level. As soon as you get the promoting at work, drive the new car, move to the new house, start your own business they will try to bring you down, or turn against you.

That's why you should always be happy when someone walks away from your life.

Only people who really care about you will be happy with your achievements.

7- "Before you post that third selfie of the day, remember: You are not a model; you are just someone with ten editing apps on your phone."

If you are not making money as a digital influencer, do you really need to post so much on social media?

People don't care where you go, what you have for breakfast, or who you hang with. Everyone is pretty busy fighting their own battles in life, and constantly showing up on people's social media feeds just makes you look like a narcissist.

And remember, people close to you know how you look in real life.

8- "SOME PEOPLE YOU WANT TO BE PART OF YOUR STORY ARE JUST MEANT TO BE THERE FOR A CHAPTER."

Friends are the most overrated thing in our modern society. It's a scam.

Just check the gallery of photos on your phone or the Facebook posts that you used to tag on it. How many of those people are still in your life? How many of them have disappointed you?

Having people around you, it's great. We are social beings. However, don't get too attached to anybody. People change. You will change. If you are lucky, some of them will just become a sweet memory every time you decide to take a trip down memory lane.

However, remember that your "Ride or Die" today can become a "backstabber" tomorrow. Your "Best Friend Forever" now can be someone suing you tomorrow.

9- "STOP GIVING CPR TO DEAD SITUATIONS."

S ome things are just beyond salvaging.

That ex, who cheated on you twice and is now trying to get back into your life. That friend that didn't pay your money back and is going around talking behind your back. Or when you tried your best and didn't get that promotion at work again.

Let it die. Sometimes, dead is better.

10- "Cut people off from your life when they are the ones handing you the scissors."

P eople don't change overnight. They usually give signs that we tend to ignore. Don't wait to see how red a flag can get.

That friend that is never there when you need them.
The loving relationship that turned toxic.
That family member that doesn't know boundaries.
The coworker that doesn't respect you.

Don't be afraid to be alone. Don't wait to cut tomorrow, someone that you can cut from your life today.

11- "IF YOU DON'T HAVE HATERS, NO ONE KNOWS WHO YOU ARE."

Celebrate your haters. You probably earn it.

The most "blended" and uninteresting people in the world are the ones that go around pleasing everybody. They kiss everyone's asses and are afraid to speak their own opinions.

Exciting and attractive people have that "Big Dick Energy" when they enter a room. They usually cause strong reactions in other people: love, hate, admiration, respect, and an uncontrollable desire to punch them in the faces.

12-"Not everything in life is a lesson. Sometimes you just fail." -Dwight Schrute – The Office

We love to ignore red flags, and only when we look back on our decisions do we realize the warning signs were there all along.

Maybe you shouldn't remortgage the house or take a loan for that trip to Paris. Or had pizza instead of the salad, or have a cheeseburger for the third time this week.

Ordered that fourth bottle of wine? Lease that sports car?

Do you really thing marrying that crazy bitch just because she is a beast in the bedroom, or that lazy guy just because of his nine- inches cock is going to give you a lifetime of happiness?

Some people will fail just because they are born on the wrong side of the tracks. Nobody can choose the circumstances in which they are born. But sometimes, you just ask for it.

13- "FOLLOW YOUR HEART, BUT ALWAYS TAKE YOUR BRAIN WITH YOU."

Your heart can be easily deceived; a nice smile, six-pack abs, and a big penis on a jobless guy with a criminal record. Big boobs and a nice ass on a narcissistic girl with murderess tendencies. The alcoholic friend that invites you for only one beer. Your heart will always push you to make the worst decisions.

Follow your heart, be present, and live the moment. However, trust your gut feeling; it usually says things like Don't drink and drive. Keep your nose clean. Sign a prenup. Don't rush to get married to someone who is coming out of a fifth divorce.

14 - "You have better things to do with your time than work your 9-5 job."

We all have bills to pay, and having a job is essential for survival.

However, no one ever got rich by working a 9 to 5 dead-end job.

Working a dead-end job is making someone's dream become reality.

See your 9-5 only as a pathway to achieve your goals.

Don't let your dreams take a backseat in your priority list.

15 - "DON'T TRUST 'LOVE' AT THE FIRST FUCK."

G ood sex can cloud your judgment of people.

It is difficult to see flaws in someone if that person just gave you the best orgasm of your life last night.

Don't be fooled by amazing blow jobs or sex with more acrobatics than a Cirque de Soleil presentation.

Take your time when you are meeting someone new, and make sure that this person has the basic requirement to be a decent human being, things like a stable job, mental health, and a clean criminal record.

16 - "Life is 10% what happens to you, and 90% how much money you have."

People who say money can't buy happiness have no idea where to shop.

Money opens doors and makes your life infinitely easier. You can't be creative when you are worried about feeding your family. You can't work towards your dream business project when you must juggle two jobs so you can afford to pay rent at the end of the month. It's difficult to work out and take care of your body when you spend hours on public transportation and can't afford expensive organic food.

Being poor is like starting a race when the others are already approaching the finish line. However, it's not a death sentence. It's unfair, but if you want to achieve your goals and make your dream come true, you must put in an astronomical effort.

Going to bed late, waking up early, making the extra hours. You will have to do extraordinary things to enjoy an extraordinary life.

17-"They are them. We are us. Fuck them all."

Prioritize only the people who treat you as a priority.

The ones that are there when you need them the most.

The ones that dream with you.

The ones that believe in you even when you are not able to believe in yourself.

The ones that show up even though they have nothing to gain.

The real ones.

The rest can go fuck themselves.

18-"SHUT UP ABOUT THE THINGS THAT YOU LOVE."

Some people will be your friends as long as you are on the same level or worse than them.

However, they will start to hate you as soon as your situation in life improves because your success is a reminder of their failure. Others just want you to fail.

In the social media era, we feel the need to share and overshare all our accomplishments. However, we might just be attracting unwanted attention and jealousy. That amazing relationship, the job promotion, the new house and the new car, the dream vacation. Stop advertising your success and become busy enjoying it.

19-"YOU DON'T HAVE TO POST IT TO PROVE IT."

First of all, nobody cares. People are just too busy failing in their own lives.

If you find something you love that makes you happy, shut up about it. Why would you want to attract unwanted attention?

The job promotion, the new house, the amazing partner. Keep it for yourself and enjoy.

20- "STOP BEING A "HUMAN DOING" AND START BEING A HUMAN BEING."

We live in a society that glamorizes multitasking to maximize material gains. The problem of embracing this philosophy is that we spend our most valuable asset: time. To be able to afford things that we don't need and don't truly make us happy.

It's time to change this perception and start to embrace a lifestyle that enables us to experience the things that really make us happy, our families, friends, and a career that gives us joy.

Do less and live more. Buy less and enjoy more. Rush less and experience more.

21- "IT'S OKAY TO BE THE VILLAIN IN SOMEONE ELSE'S STORY."

Stop worrying about what other people think about you. It says more about them than you. People will hurt you and act like you hurt them.

If you are the villain in someone else's story, make sure they are the clown in yours.

22-"DO WHAT YOU CAN, WITH WHAT YOU HAVE, WHERE YOU ARE."

THEODORE ROOSEVELT

Jeff Bezos started the empire that is Amazon today in his garage. Don't wait until next year, or when you get the job, pay off the house, get married, until the kids grow up. Start small, start slow, start with the little you have, start with nothing, just start.

In the words of the great Martin Luther King Jr.:

"If you can't fly, then run; if you can't run, then walk, if you can't walk, then crawl, but whatever you do, you. have to keep moving forward."

23- "WORRY IS A MISUSE OF IMAGINATION."

Worrying about a situation gives us the fake feeling of doing something about it. However, that couldn't be further from the truth. Worrying about something that we can't control only increases our anxiety level and robs us of inner peace.

The reality is that there is very little in life that we can control, and one of the things we can actually control is our reactions to the challenges that life throws at us.

Focus on your mental health and guard your inner peace at all costs.

24-"Do not wait for the perfect time and place to enter, for you are already onstage."

There will never be a right time. Stop waiting until next year, until your birthday, until next Monday.

Do it now. Quit your dead-end job, break up from that toxic relationship, start your own business, move to another city. Say "I love you" to that special person. Say "Fuck you" to that "special" person.

Life is happening now.

25-"A GOOD ASS-KISSER IS USUALLY AN EVEN BETTER BACK-STABBER."

Don't be deceived by words from people who are constantly trying to show off how nice they are.

Usually ass-kissers have an agenda. They want something from you.

People kissing your ass today are just waiting the for opportunity to stab you in the back tomorrow.

26-"If life doesn't break you today, don't worry. It will try again tomorrow."

L ife is like a roller-coaster with its ups and downs. Just because you are on top today doesn't mean you will stay there forever.

You may be the one that enjoys the promotion today but get fired before the month closes. You can buy the house and the sports car now and file for bankruptcy next year. You can marry that special person in the summer and sign the divorce papers by next winter. Be humble and get off of your high horse.

Life can be a real bitch, and tomorrow is only a day away.

27- "Multitasking is just doing twice as much as you should, half as well as you could."

In recent years, the myth of multitasking has been debunked. However, many people still believe and practice it.

Multitasking is a recipe for spreading yourself too thin and achieving poor results in all your tasks.

Focus on one thing at a time. The word "Multitasking" was probably created by a manager who was short on staff.

28-"Better Done Than Perfect." – ChatGPT

You never will achieve perfection in anything. Being a perfectionist can lead you to inertia to act on your plans. There will never be a perfect time to start something.

Don't wait until the stars align, or until you have more time, get married, or until the kids grow up. Do it without the money, without the support from friends and family.

The feeling of accomplishment is better than the regret from procrastination. Just do it.

29-"LIFE BETTER BE A DESTINATION BECAUSE THIS JOURNEY SUCKS."

Don't believe all that people say. They just want to sound wise. The journey and the process of achieving a goal and making your dreams come true is painful. The sooner you understand this, the sooner you will achieve all your dreams. Embrace the process, embrace the pain.

Your bitchy wife or asshole husband will never get better. Your ungrateful children will never appreciate anything you do. That obnoxious coworker or abusive boss will never change. So, get a divorce, quit now, move on.

30-"WHEN LIFE KNOCKS YOU DOWN, STAY THERE AND TAKE A NAP."

What can you do when things are going downhill?

Sometimes, hitting rock bottom is the only way up.

Visualizing the worst-case scenario can take away all the power of worry and anxiety.

So what? You lost the job. Your partner is sleeping with your best friend. The bank is taking back the car. You have to move out by Monday. Your pregnancy test is positive. Fuck it.

There is nothing you can do about it apart from self-indulge in anxiety. Relax, turn your phone off, take a nap, rest, and start the battle over tomorrow.

31-"LIFE DOESN'T USE LUBRICANT."

Life has no favorites. It fucks everybody up without discrimination.

Stop playing the victim part. We all come from dysfunctional families, with way less money than we want, and it doesn't matter how hot we are; nobody is happy with their own bodies.

So, stop throwing your pity parties and start taking responsibility for your own happiness.

32-"YOU'RE ONLY AS GOOD AS YOUR LAST MISTAKE."

D on't be naïve. People love, care, and want to be around you. Until you fuck up.

Actually, you don't even need to fuck up. If you lose your job, get sick for more than one week, or even need a ride for more than one day, chances are that your phone will probably stop ringing, and those social media notifications will dry up.

33-"Never miss a good chance to shut up." – Will Rogers.

It is a tale as old as time. "It's better to keep your mouth shut and appear stupid than open it and remove all the doubt."

Modern society tends to underestimate the power of silence. You don't need to give your opinion about every single thing.

34-"THE WORST THINGS IN YOUR LIFE PROBABLY HAVEN'T HAPPENED TO YOU YET."

And they probably never will.

Although things can always get worse, some of the things you fear the most will never come to fruition.

The worst-case scenarios that kept you up all night long didn't materialize. Overthinking makes you spend the most valuable asset that you have: TIME.

35- "YOU CAN BE REPLACED"

Are you sacrificing yourself at work or going above and beyond for that "special" person, friend, or family member? DON'T.

They will replace you at the first opportunity they have.

You definitely have to work hard and go the extra mile to achieve your goals and make your dream come true; however, do it for yourself, do it because it makes you happy, and do it if it brings you joy.

Don't kill yourself for something or someone. Remember, our most valuable asset in life is time. Spend wisely.

36-"MEDIOCRITY IN YOUR GOALS IS THE KEY TO NEVER FALLING SHORT OF YOUR EXPECTATIONS."

Sometimes, simplicity is the key to happiness.

Why open a restaurant in a neighborhood with another fifty well-stabilized places? Why ask for the number of the hottest girl at the party? Why slide to the DM's of the guy that has fucked half of your girlfriends. Why keep buying new clothes to make you feel good if what you really need to do is lose weight?

Start small, open a food truck. Ask that ugly girl with the big boob out. Smile to the nerdy guy with a stable job. Sign up for that gym membership.

37-"We are not in the same boat; some have Yachts, and some are just drowning."

Stop trying to compare yourself with everyone else. Meritocracy is a myth because none of us have the same starting point in life.

The good news is that we are all a little fucked up.

Focus on becoming the best version of yourself. Keep going steady on your path; eventually, the storm will pass, and you will arrive at your destination.

38-"REAL FRIENDSHIP IS BUILT ON A SOLID FOUNDATION OF DISLIKE OF THE SAME PEOPLE."

Nothing makes you bond with someone faster than hating the same things or the same people.

39-"BE THE REASON SOMEONE IS HORNY TODAY."

Be romantic! But understand that giving someone an orgasm is better than giving them flowers and chocolates. An epic orgasm will leave an impression that lasts longer than roses.

40-"When toxic people stop talking to you, it's like the trash took itself out."

R ejection is just protection in disguise.

Celebrate every time someone walks away from your life, when you get fired from a deadening job, when your toxic partner breaks up with you, or when that fake friend stops talking to you. It's just destiny acting in your favor.

Some people are not meant to be part of your future. They need to go so you can make space for better friends, opportunities, and a new love. Let them all go.

41-"Follow your heart, but always take your brain with you."

Your heart can be easily deceived; a nice smile, six-pack abs, and a big penis on a jobless guy with a criminal record. Big boobs and a nice ass on a narcissistic girl with murderess tendencies. The alcoholic friend that invites you for only one beer. Your heart will always push you to make the worst decisions.

Follow your heart, be present, and live the moment. However, trust your gut feeling; it usually says things like Don't drink and drive. Keep your nose clean. Sign a prenup. Don't rush to get married to someone who is coming out of a fifth divorce.

42-"BETTER AN OOPS THAN A WHAT IF."

Nobody thinks they should have worked, slept, watched more TV, or played more video games on their deathbed. So don't overthink!

Do it now, regret it later.

43-"WHEN WORK FEELS OVERWHELMING, REMEMBER THAT YOU'RE GOING TO DIE."

Remember, you are not coming out of life alive. There is a liberating feeling of acceptance. Instead of wasting all your time and energy on anxiety and fighting to fix things that can't be fixed, embrace the worst-case scenario.

Yes, you will get fired. Yes, the exam results came back positive. Yes, your partner is cheating on you. Yes, and now what? The worst came to worst. Push came to shove.

You must find the strength to pick up all the pieces and move on. The only way out is through. Keep moving, and eventually, you will get out of the situation as you have done many times before.

44-"Make yourself all honey, and the flies will devour you."

Honey attracts bees and butterflies, but it also attracts flies. Being sweet and nice can attract more people into your life.

However, you need to learn the difference between bees and flies.

The difference between the ones that deserve your sweatiness and the ones that you need to cut out from your life before it's too late.

45-"The sun comes out every day; if you can't see, it's the clouds' fault."

There is always a new day, a unique opportunity, a new job, a new friend, a new special person just around the corner. Sometimes, our vision is clouded by dark thoughts, bad memories from past experiences, and everybody's least favorite "friend" anxiety.

Remember everything that you had to go through to get here.

Take a moment to yourself, take a deep breath, analyze the situation with a fresh mind, and see the sky clear.

Until now, you have a 100% survival rate.

46-"EVERYONE HAS A CHAPTER THEY DON'T WANT TO READ OUT LOUD."

We all have a dark time in our lives that we don't even want to remember.

Emotional dependency, financial struggles, addiction, waking up naked next to someone that you have no idea who they are, emo style in high school.

So, get down from your high horse and stop being so judgmental to others.

47-"LET YOUR WEIRD LIGHT SHINE BRIGHT SO THE OTHER WEIRDOS KNOW WHERE TO FIND YOU."

Embrace your uniqueness and weirdness. It will attract all the right people to your life. Maybe your soulmate, perhaps your partner in crime.

48-"THE HARDEST THING IN LIFE IS LETTING GO OF WHAT YOU THINK IS REAL."

Sometimes, we tend to create scenarios that only exist in our minds.

Some relationships are never meant to last.

Learn to recognize the difference between a "6 pm Friday friend" and a "3 am Friend for all emergencies."

The difference between someone who will grow older with you and someone that is a really good time in bed.

The difference between someone who really needs help and someone who is a parasite in your life.

49-"SOMETIMES YOU SPEAK MUCH BETTER IN SILENCE."

Never underestimate the power of silence. You will look like the "bigger and wiser person" in an argument.

Besides, indifference is the ultimate offense to narcissist people.

Instead of overreacting or speaking words that you will regret later, ignoring someone will get the job done.

50-"People will hurt you and act like you hurt them."

This is gaslighting at its best!

Learn how to recognize someone with narcissistic tendencies. They usually feed on drama and always try to shift the blame on you.

Family, friends, co-workers, it doesn't matter; at the first sign of a toxic behavior pattern, cut them out your life immediately. You will be avoiding future drama and saving precious time in your life.

51-"WHEN TRUST IS BROKEN, SORRY MEANS NOTHING."

Do not give second chances.

Life is too short to be wasted on backstabbers, liars, and cheaters. Lose your fear of being alone. The worst kind of loneliness is the one where you are surrounded by people and still feel empty.

Normalizing telling people to fuck off from your life more often.

52-"Be careful who you trust. Salt and sugar look the same."

R ome wasn't built in one day, and neither is trust.

Maybe you shouldn't consider a best friend that person you met last night at 3 am when you were drunk at a bar.

Perhaps you shouldn't move in with the person you have been seeing for less than two weeks. Maybe you shouldn't tell all your secrets to that nice person in your department whom you have been working with for less than a month.

53- "IT'S NEVER TOO LATE TO FAIL."

The secret to success in life is not to be afraid of failure.

You will miss 100% of the shots that you don't take. So, fail, fail hard, and then fail again.

Eventually, you will get what you want or even something much better. Fail all the way to your success.

54- "Doing nothing is very hard to do... you never know when you're finished."

Procrastination can be very addictive, a never-ending circle.

Getting stuff done is hard. Losing weight is hard. Opening your own business is hard. Getting that degree is hard. Cutting ties with loved ones, even though they are toxic to you, is hard. Working toward your goals is very hard.

However, being fat and getting sick is hard, and staying in a dead-end job is hard. Being poor is very hard. Let's be honest: watching people you hate or your peers succeed is even harder.

Choose your "hard" wisely.

55-"THE BEST THINGS IN LIFE ARE ACTUALLY REALLY EXPENSIVE."

The 300 dollars that you save by buying that crappy computer is not worth it. The cheap clothes that you buy today will not last long. The cheaper plane ticket ends up costing more than a regular ticket.

The most important resource that you have is time. Time is money, so spend it consciously.

Outsource mindless work that steals your time, and focus on what is really important to achieve your goals.

56-"When tempted to fight fire with fire, remember that the Fire Department usually uses water."

Don't start that bar fight or that well-deserved road rage, nor reply to the text message that looks like an essay.

It's never worth it to match the mental health state of a loser who is trying to ruin your day.

Silence is extremely powerful and the best reply to an idiot.

57- "STEPPING OUT OF YOUR COMFORT ZONE IS A GOOD WAY TO APPRECIATE HOW NICE AND COMFY IT IS."

Be adventurous, bold, and brave. Don't be afraid to take chances and run towards your challenges. That doesn't mean you should be stupid and overreact in every single situation.

Sometimes, you shouldn't break up a solid two-year committed relationship because of the amazing sex that you are having with your affair. Maybe you shouldn't quit your job and start that business without researching the marketplace. Maybe you shouldn't invest all your savings in cryptocurrency.

Be laser-focused and strategic about your goals. Take calculated risks, and always have a plan B, C, and D because things never go as expected.

58-"SOMETIMES YOU JUST HAVE TO ACCEPT THAT SOME PEOPLE ARE SHITTY HUMANS AND STOP TRYING TO SEE THE GOOD THAT ISN'T THERE."

Sometimes, you need to call a Spade a Spade. There is no sugar coating. People just don't change overnight. A cheater will always betray you; a dishonest person will do dishonest things. A hater will always hate. It's up to you to end their cycle in your life.

As your grandmother used to say: "Fool me once, shame on you. Fool me twice, shame on me."

59-"YOU ARE ALWAYS A TRENDING TOPIC IN YOUR HATER'S LIFE."

It doesn't matter how hard you try to be nice or change people's opinions. Your haters will always find a way to bitch about you.

Live your life, and don't care about their opinions. Give them a solid reason to hate you.

60-"Follow your brain. Your heart is stupid as fuck."

Don't trust your heart. The amazing sex and smooth talk from that special person is clouding your judgment.

Falling in love with someone is one of the best feelings that you can experience. However, you should have some standards before falling hopelessly in love with that special person.

A partner can make or break a person. Being tied up with the wrong partner can ruin you emotionally and financially.

Before your fall in love with a girl that has terrific boobs or that guy with a big dick, make sure they have a job or at least some professional plans for the future. Or maybe something simpler, like a clean criminal record, can be a good start.

61-"Sometimes the short and best answer is No. The long answer, and second-best answer, is: Oh, Fuck No!"

The most important thing you will ever learn in your life is to say "no" to people. Human beings are social beings, and social norms have taught us to be polite in order to live in harmony with each other.

So, we tend to say yes to situations, even though we don't want to, just to avoid confrontation or making other people upset. We waste time on things that are not important, people who don't really care about us instead of investing our time towards achieving our goals and dreams.

However, time is our most precious resource, and every time we say yes to something, we are saying no to something else.

62-"WHEN PEOPLE TREAT YOU LIKE THEY DON'T CARE, BELIEVE THEM."

There are more than 8 billion people in the world. Do you really need to be running after people who don't care about you?

Stop ignoring the signs and microaggressions. People who care and like you don't play games with your feelings. They make time; they put the effort to make things happen, and they show up when you need them.

63-"THE MEANING OF LIFE IS TO FIND YOUR GIFT."

Everyone is born with a gift. Some people excel in communication, arts, and math. Nowadays, people can excel and monetize absolutely everything. Some are doing silly dances on social media, and others are "performing" on adult platforms like "Onlyfans."

In a world where people are becoming millionaires by selling photos of their feet or jars with their farts, don't be afraid to explore your unique "gifts."

Embrace your uniqueness.

64-"YOU ARE ALWAYS A TRENDING TOPIC IN YOUR HATER'S LIFE."

It doesn't matter how hard you try to be nice or change people's opinions. Your haters will always find a way to bitch about you.

Live your life, and don't care about their opinions.

Give them a solid reason to hate you.

65-"BE READY TO LICK THE SPOON IF YOU STIR THE SHIT POT."

Trust your instincts. That gut feeling that sends us a sign when something is not right. Or just use some old-fashioned common sense. Avoid putting yourself into situations that you know are going to end up badly. Stay away from people who are trouble.

Maybe, just maybe, you shouldn't cheat on your partner or "borrow" that money/ or thing that doesn't belong to you. Or drive after that fourth shot of tequila.

66-"Don't be a heartless person. Just learn how to use your heart less."

As life goes on, people will disappoint you, betray you, and even hurt you. Most people will tend to close themselves off to new opportunities in life, which can lead to loneliness and unhappiness.

Don't let life's disappointments make you unable to use your heart. Use these experiences as knowledge and learn how to use your heart in a smart way.

67-"EXPECT NOTHING, APPRECIATE EVERYTHING."

There is nothing wrong in wanting only the best in life.

However, "Toxic Positivity" is real. We fall into the trap of entitlement, leading us to a constant state of anxiety, waiting always for the best results, and disappointment and frustration when things don't happen the way that we expected.

Gratitude for all that you already have erases this anxiety, and once you stop expecting things, you will always be pleasantly surprised by destiny.

68-"A YEAR FROM NOW, YOU WILL WISH YOU HAD STARTED TODAY."

The best time to start something was yesterday. The next best time is today.

A year from now, you will wish to had started that diet, started going to the gym, learned a new skill, and opened your own business. You wished you had walked out of that toxic relationship.

And when it comes to relationships, don't wait to tell someone to fuck off tomorrow if you can tell them to fuck off today.

69-"WE ALL KNOW SOMEONE WHO SPEAKS FLUENT SHIT."

We all know someone like this. Avoid these people in your life because if you hang around them for too long, you will start to speak the same language.

70-"Doing nothing is better than being busy doing nothing."

We live in a society that glamorizes being busy, as theoretically, being busy means accomplishing more. Accomplishing more means more money, more success, and more material gain. Even when we are not doing anything, we are busy thinking and worrying about stuff.

However, are all those tasks on our "to-do list" moving us towards accomplishing our goals, or are they actually just delaying them? According to the "80-20 rule," a familiar saying asserts that 80% of outcomes (or outputs) result from 20% of all causes (or inputs) for any given event. This means that 80% of our results come from only 20% of our efforts.

How many meetings have we had to attend that never led to anything? How many bad dates did we go through only to meet the one in the supermarket line?

Stop being afraid to say no. Stop running around just to feel busy. Stop overthinking a situation just to feel like you are doing something about it. Value your time. It's your most precious asset.

71-"CANCEL YOUR SUBSCRIPTION TO OTHER PEOPLE'S ISSUES"

You already have to deal with your own drama. Why get invested in someone else's for free?

How much time do we waste involved in battles that are not yours? Precious time that you could spend becoming a better version of ourselves or wrestling towards our goals.

Start to say no to invitations, don't reply to texts, don't answer phone calls. Focus on investing all your time, resources, and efforts in the most important relationship you will have in your life, which is with yourself.

72-"Others can't use you if you're useless."

We all want something from people around us—friendship, love, validation. However, there are some people who want to use you. Some people want to abuse you. But nobody can take advantage of you if you can't provide any value to them.

Start saying "no" to people and watch the ones that are around you just for personal gain disappear.

73-"According to Astronomy, when you wish upon a star, you're actually a few million years too late. That star is dead."

Sooner or later, we all realize that life is not a fairytale. Sometimes, it's more like a horror movie or a drama.

Wishing will never bring your dreams to life. Find your purpose, and focus on achieving your goals daily; if you fail, get back to it immediately.

Run, walk, crawl, do whatever you can to keep moving toward your dreams. Go the extra mile, do another rep, try to be 1% better than yesterday, and when you least expect, you will live on your own fairytale.

74-"Reach for the stars. Follow your dreams. Live with your parents."

Don't be ashamed of where you are in your journey, and stop comparing yourself to others.

Don't be afraid to start small. Go back to school, get that entry-level job, start your own business in your parent's garage, just start!

Because the best day to start something was yesterday, and the second-best day is today.

And why are you thinking about leaving your parent's house in this economy?

75-"The universe doesn't give a shit about you."

The universe has no favorites. Stop blaming life, other people, and even destiny for everything that happens in your life.

Take the steering wheel of your life, and be responsible to build the road to your destiny.

There is nobody after you, or does the world have an agenda against you. The reality is that people are too busy dealing with their own drama.

76-"TODAY WILL BE A DAY LIKE EVERY OTHER DAY."

Nothing will ever change in your life if you do the same thing today that you did yesterday, the day before, last week, last month, and last year.

If you really want change, be bold and have the courage to do everything that has been in the back of your mind: ask that hot girl out, slide into that special guy's DM, shave your hair, apply for your dream job even though you don't have all the requirements.

77-"If it requires fake smiling, it's probably not worth it."

L ife is too short for fake wine, fake cheese, and fake people.

Don't go to that family gathering where your alcoholic aunt will make comments about your weight. Tell that toxic coworker to "Kiss Your Ass" instead of "Good Morning." Inform your asshole partner that they have a week to "Fuck off" from your life.

78-"If you truly believe in yourself, you have no need to convince others."

Once you know who you are, believing in yourself gets easier.

Once you believe in yourself, you will be free from other people's opinions and judgments because you will just not care, the most liberating feeling is not caring about what people think about you.

There is something special about people who really know who they are. They carry themselves differently. They are unapologetic confident and do not need to feel accepted by others.

Once you believe in yourself unconditionally, you will never feel the need for approval from anyone.

79-"THE HUMAN EXISTENCE WITHOUT WINE ISN'T HUMAN EXISTENCE."

What was the first miracle of Jesus in the Bible? Did he resurrect the dead? Did he make people who are blind see? Did he make the crippled walk?

No! He turned water into wine. That says something.

80-"What doesn't kill you makes you bitter and terrible to be around."

Don't ever neglect your mental health. Are you really upset about something that just happened, or was it just a trigger for a deep-seated trauma?

Look for professional help if you can, or do a self-assessment and try to clean up all the skeletons in your closet. Don't give power to the villains from your past to influence your future.

Some people will not be part of your life story; they are meant to stay for a brief chapter.

81-"The only thing your failures have in common is you."

Stop complaining about every single bad thing that happens to you. People around you will realize that all the drama in your life has the same common denominator:

You.

82- "Find the one thing you love and shut up about it"

That goes for everything in your life. That small local Italian restaurant that gives you unlimited garlic rolls. That hot girl who is a beast in bed and loves cooking. That hot sensitive guy with a 9-inch cock that is rough in bed but wants to cuddle after you have had five orgasms in a row.

People will ruin everything. Just keep it to yourself and enjoy your secret twisted treasures.

83-"FOREVER COMES WITH AN EXPIRATION DAY."

Nothing lasts forever. That passionate relationship with your spouse. That best friend who is closer than family. The joy of working on the job that you always wanted. Or even the bad things like the pain from a broken heart. The never-ending cold, lonely nights. That toxic relationship that you can't wait to get out.

It will all pass.

Read all the contracts before you sign. Keep all the receipts and screenshots. You never know when you will need to get a lawyer and file a lawsuit against somebody who used to be your BFF (Best Friend Forever.)

84- "Dreams are like rainbows. Only idiots chase them.

Only idiots go after their dreams without a plan.

Be intentional, write a business plan, set a deadline, and reassess and reevaluate your goals.

Otherwise, your dreams will be nothing more than dreams.

85-"IF YOUR RELATIONSHIP GIVES YOU LEMONS, SQUEEZE SOMEONE ELSE."

When life give you lemons on your relationship, return them immediately, and don't hide your emotions.

Breakups are hard. Allow yourself to grieve the end of the relationship, but move on fast.

Don't waste your time trying to resurrect a dead relationship. It will only make you lose your self-esteem, and the little respect that your ex-partner has for you.

As your old grandmother used to say: "The best way to get over someone is to get under someone else."

86-"What is a fart if you already shit yourself."

There are situations where you can't do anything about it to change the outcome. That's the moment where the only attitude you can have it's a "Fuck it" attitude.

That "Fuck It" attitude is liberating. It saves you time in giving CPR to dead situations. It frees your mind of the anxiety and guilt.

It motivates you to go from a freezing state of fear and disappointment to a must "move on" mindset, and in the long run, you will understand the importance of keeping moving no matter what.

87-"BE THE REASON SOMEONE SMILES TODAY OR THE REASON SOMEONE DRINKS, IS HORNY, OR IS AFRAID."

Whoever you choose to be in life, don't choose to be someone who is uninteresting.

Be yourself in all your glory. Go the extra mile in everything you do in life. Let people know who you are by being the best version of the person you want to be.

Draw the boundary line for that toxic coworker or family member. Impress that special person by going the extra mile sexually and emotionally. Leave a long-lasting impression.

Give your enemies and haters a reason to hate you even more. Let them know better than to try to fuck with you.

88-"NO EXPECTATIONS, NO DISAPPOINTMENTS."

We are all victims of victims, trying our best not to fail in our own lives.

People will disappoint you, and you will eventually disappoint people. So, stop expecting others to make you happy, help you start a project, or motivate you to change.

Don't give anybody power over your life. Be responsible for your own happiness; you are the only one capable of making your dreams come true.

89-"There is no limit to what you can be if you lie to yourself."

You can become what you believe. According to quantum physics, there is no limit to what we can become.

However, believing in yourself can be a problem because most of us have to deal with childhood trauma, emotional wounds, low self-esteem, and ever-present anxiety. Our subconscious mind is powerful and can bring to life whatever we believe, for better or worse, and best way to get over our past traumas is to feed positivity into our subconscious mind.

So, yes, you had a fucked-up childhood, your love life sucks, and you hate your job. But instead of constantly ruminating and echoing the negativity, therefore creating more and more of the same, swift your focus into positive things. Believe you can transform your life.

It won't be easy at first, but as soon as your subconscious mind accepts your new ideas, your conscious mind will open up to new possibilities, allowing you to create an exciting future.

90-"If it is important to you, you will find a way. If not, you'll find an excuse."

Only choose people that choose you.

Someone who really cares will always find a way, even when it is to bail you out of jail.

91-"You See a Person's True Colors When You Are No Longer Beneficial to Their Life."

Human beings are sociable beings by nature. It has been imprinted on our brains since the beginning of our existence. It was a death sentence to be isolated by the tribe in the Stone Age. The isolated human wouldn't be able to hunt and defend himself against the dangerous beasts that walked on earth at the time, and we also have a primal instinct to mate.

However, nowadays, we have to make sure that all our relationships are a two-way street. An easy way to see if your friends are real is to say no to them.

Try it; stop loaning money, giving rides, and showing up for every single stupid gathering. Or try to start asking for money, asking for a ride, saying you are sick for more than one week, and see if they will stick with you.

92-"PARENTS NOTICE YOUR FAKE FRIENDS BEFORE YOU DO."

Do your parents have a divine infinity of wisdom? Most likely not. However, they have lived longer, and by default, they have seen more assholes than you. That makes it easier for them to see and identify red flags on your friends.

You should definitely take into consideration their judgment about your newest "best friend forever."

93-"YOU DON'T HAVE TO ATTEND EVERY ARGUMENT YOU'RE INVITED TO."

Choose your battles wisely. Some people are just simply not worthy. Why would you spend your time and energy going down to their lower level?

Silence is power. Sometimes, the best answer to an argument is indifference. It shows that you are capable of controlling your emotions, puts you in a position of superiority, and makes you look like the bigger person.

94-"YOU HAVE SURVIVED 100% OF YOUR WORST DAYS. THIS TOO SHALL PASS."

When worst comes to worst, it's easy to feel like this is it, this is the end. However, if you check your track record, you will realize that you have survived every single bad situation you have encountered.

You might have crawled out of it. You might have had your heart and soul broken, and maybe even survived physical harm. You might still be dealing with it. But you have survived, after all.

So, when things are going downhill, encourage yourself by looking back at your past and remembering that you already went through worse before and came out on top.

95-"Speak when you are angry, and this will make the best speech you'll forever regret."

Don't be a slave of your emotions.

Words are powerful, and they can't be taken back once they are spoken. People can forgive you but will never forget how you made them feel.

Even though some stupid people deserve your wrath, it is better to ignore them by using the power of silence and indifference.

96-"Never underestimate the importance of being outstandingly mediocre."

The pressure of performing well every single task in your life can be exhausting and leads to constant anxiety.

Don't be ashamed of where you are on the journey, and often take time out for yourself, analyze, reevaluate your plans, or even indulge yourself once in a while.

There is nothing wrong with a C+ on a test, needing a whole bottle of wine after your kids go to bed, or spending the weekend watching football on the sofa with a beer in your hand.

97-"When your life goes up, you can fall from a new height."

Don't think too highly of yourself. Life is made of ups and downs. Everything that goes up must come down.

Some people are anxiously waiting for your fall. So be nice to everyone you encounter on your way up because you might meet them again on your way down.

98-"EVERYONE SUCKS AT SOMETHING."

Don't be intimidated by anyone. God has no favorites.

Nobody can be good at everything, and we are all fighting our own battles. That hot girl you are jealous of is probably not as funny as you. The hot guy that you are jealous of probably has a small penis.

The only person you should try to be better than is the person you were yesterday.

Forget about the competition and keep moving forward.

99-"New beginnings are often disguised as painful endings."

Don't ever fear when cycles come to an end in your life. A terrible breakup, a friend that walks out of your life, being fired from a job. Although painful, some endings are only life making way to new and better things in your future.

You will never change your life professionally without being fired from that job. You will never meet the love of your life if you are stuck in that relationship. You will never have new friends in your life if you were still attached to toxic people.

Don't be afraid of losing something or someone.

Always welcome the "new" into your life.

100- "NO" – ROSA PARKS. 1955.

There is a point in our lives where enough is enough when you become sick and tired of being sick and tired.

It's scary and extremely uncomfortable but also an important turning point. That is when you quit the job, say no to an abuser, put an end to a relationship, pack your things, and leave.

This is when your new life begins, starting with a quiet "no" or with a loud "Fuck you."

101-"It takes thirty-seven muscles to frown, but it takes zero muscles to shut the fuck up."

Never underestimate the power of silence. It puts you automatically in a position of superiority against narcissist.

In an argument silence can make the other person question the power of their own words.

A stoic reply can make your opponent doubt themselves.

102-"Before you judge someone else, try to keep in mind that you're probably a piece of shit too."

Nobody likes self-righteousness. We all have flaws, and when push comes to shave, we are capable of the most despicable things.

So, before you open your mouth to judge someone, take a good look at yourself. Chances are that you would probably do the same or much worse if you were in their position.

103-"HATE TAKES TOO MUCH ENERGY. JUST PRETEND THEY ARE DEAD ALREADY."

Why are you still hating that ex-girlfriend just because she said you would never amount to anything in life?

Why are you still hating that boyfriend who cheated on you with your best friend?

Why are you still holding grudges against your drunk parents and jealous siblings?

Let them all go. Clear this heavy energy from your life. Forgive them, not because they deserve forgiveness, but because you deserve peace.

104-"WE ALL KNOW SOMEONE WHO SPEAKS FLUENT SHIT."

We all know someone like this.

Avoid these people in your life because if you hang around them for too long, you will start to speak the same language.

105-"YOU CAN'T CONTROL EVERYTHING. YOUR HAIR WAS PUT ON YOUR HEAD TO REMIND YOU OF THAT."

Stop trying to control everything and everyone around you. The sooner you learn this, the happier you will be.

The need to control just leads you to two things: anxiety and frustration.

Instead, try to control the only thing that you actually can control, which is how you react to the things that happen to you.

106-"Only dead fish go with the flow."

Stop following every single trend.

Stop competing to be average.

Stop trying to be accepted in social circles by changing who you are.

Embrace your uniqueness and embrace who you are.

By being your true self, you will piss off the ones who shouldn't be in your life and attract the right people into your world.

107-"Some people fell from heaven, just like Satan."

Stop ignoring the red flags, and don't trust your judgment based on how hot someone is or how good they are in bed.

Sometimes the crazy bitch with the big boobs or the dumb jock with the 9-inch cock will not make the best life partners.

108-"The only thing that counts in life is results, not reasons for not doing it."

The only outcomes that matter are results. Positive or negative results are all that matter.

If the results are positive, it's an accomplishment for you; if they are negative, it can be a valuable lesson.

However, the one thing nobody cares about is the reasons why you didn't try.

109- "Social Media is a great place to look at pictures of the fake lives of all the people you hate."

After the invention of image filters, nobody is ugly anymore.

Pay attention to what type of online content you consume. Social media is designed to be addictive, and it's able to destroy your self-esteem.

Don't believe in what people post. Nobody wakes up every day looking fabulous and full of motivation.

People are not as happy, funny, or intelligent as they appear on their social media feeds.

110-"If You Can't Say Anything Nice...Make It Funny."

You don't need to give your opinion about every single thing.

However, sometimes, it is impossible to keep our mouths shut about certain things. That's where sarcasm comes in handy.

Being fluent in sarcasm makes everything better. You can be brutally mean, and people will think you are just trying to be funny.

111-"You Only Die Once."

You will have to live today with yesterday's decisions.

Maybe you shouldn't have that third slice of pizza or order that fourth shot of tequila.

The same goes for telling your boss to fuck off, dropping out school, going on a date with someone that is already in a relationship, or getting that tattoo on your face.

112-"TODAY IS THE FIRST DAY OF THE REST OF YOUR LIFE. BUT SO WAS YESTERDAY, AND LOOK HOW THAT TURNED OUT."

Your life doesn't magically change because it's your birthday, the first day of the year, or simply because it's Monday.

If you don't want to achieve the same results over and over again. Don't be afraid to try something different and take risks.

Turn off that dammed TV. Put your phone down and go work out. Apply for that job. Send the text to your crush even though that person is in a serious relationship with someone else.

113-"LIFE IS A BITCH, AND THEN YOU DIE."

Stop thinking you are special. Stop thinking you are "the chosen one," like the main character in a bad 90's movie. You are extraordinarily average, and life is merciless to everyone.

If you are not born rich, you will have to get a job that you hate. You will eventually have family and friends that will disappoint you. Then, if you are lucky, you will grow older, your knees and your lower back will let you down, and then you will die.

If you really want to change your life and have a better future, you must be ready to do extraordinary things. Things that average people are not willing to do: go to bed late, wake up early, work extra hours, do the extra set of reps at the gym, eat that healthy food you hate.

114-"A YEAR FROM NOW, YOU WILL WISH YOU HAD STARTED TODAY."

The best time to start something was yesterday. The next best time is today.

A year from now, you will wish to had started that diet, started going to the gym, learned a new skill, and opened your own business. You wished you had walked out of that toxic relationship.

And when it comes to relationships, don't wait to tell someone to fuck off tomorrow if you can tell them to fuck off today.

115-"If you live for people's acceptance, you will die from their rejection."

S top giving others power over your life. Stop seeking acceptance and approval.

Embrace your uniqueness, and learn how to love yourself.

We come into this world alone, and we will leave this world alone. Everything else is optional.

116-"Don't be a heartless person. Just learn how to use your heart less."

As life goes on, people will disappoint you, betray you, and even hurt you.

Most people will tend to close themselves to new opportunities in life, which can lead to loneliness and unhappiness.

Don't let life's disappointments make you unable to use your heart.

Use these experiences as knowledge and learn how to use your heart in a smart way.

117-"You can't control everything. Your hair was put on your head to remind you of that."

Stop trying to control everything and everyone around you. The sooner you learn this, the happier you will be.

The need to control just leads you to two things: anxiety and frustration.

Instead, try to control the only thing that you actually can control, which is how you react to the things that happen to you.

118-"LITERALLY, NO ONE CARES."

Have you ever stopped doing something you wanted because you were worried about what people would think?

The truth of the matter is that no one cares. People are too busy failing in their own lives.

Everyone has an annoying, lazy husband, a bitchy wife, an incompetent child, an asshole coworker, an annoying a boss, a crazy neighbor to worry about it.

119-"JUST BECAUSE PEOPLE ACCEPT YOU AS YOU ARE DOESN'T MEAN THEY'VE ABANDONED HOPE YOU'LL IMPROVE."

Nowadays, common sense is like a superpower, and due to our current political correctness climate, we are afraid of telling people off. This leads to more idiots walking around unchecked. Make sure you are not one of them.

Just because your family and friends have put up with your shit for years doesn't mean they lost the hope that one day you will finally get a grip and start to behave like a normal human being.

120-"Some people are just like diapers. Self-absorbed and full of shit.

I t takes time to realize when someone is full of shit. We usually give them the benefit of the doubt and classify them as a quirk or eccentric, but they start to stink sooner or later.

Learn how to identify these kinds of people and unceremoniously cut them out of your life

121-"Don't cry because it's over. Smile because if you don't, everyone will ask you what's wrong."

Do you really want to explain to someone why you ignore all the red flags in a toxic relationship? Or that you have to keep that job that you hate because you were born into poverty.

Most people don't care about your problems, and others are happy that you have them to begin with.

Find professional help, someone who is capable of giving you proper guidance and support, but avoid curiosity and unwanted attention in your life.

Keep pretending that you still have mental health and smile at everyone.

122-"Your friends are God's apology to you for the family that you were born in." - Tennessee Williams

Many of us had drunk parents or had some severe case of sibling rivalry. It doesn't matter if you were born rich or poor; all families are dysfunctional in one way or another.

However, somewhere down the line, life allows us to choose the special people we want to keep as part of our story.

Forgive your dysfunctional family members; at the end of the day, we are all victims of victims.

Focus on using your time and energy on the people that really matter in your life.

123-"LIFE IS WHAT HAPPENS WHEN YOU'RE BUSY READING INSPIRATIONAL QUOTES."

Sometimes, the best way to learn about life is to be punched right in the face by it.

The best way to learn about love is to have your heart broken. The best way to learn about investments is when you lose all your money by investing in crypto.

Just be brave and go out there and live, fuck things up, then look back and learn from it.

Earn and be proud of your stripes, thick skin, and scars.

124-"When the Going Gets Tough, the Tough Get Tougher."

When things get bad, the only way out is through. There is no other way around.

It will be ugly and painful. It will cost you blood, sweat, and tears. The sooner you acknowledge this, the easier it will be for you to navigate the choppy waters of success.

Don't be afraid to fail. Learn from your mistakes, bad experiences, and assholes that cross your path.

125-"QUITTERS NEVER WIN, AND WINNERS NEVER QUIT TALKING ABOUT HOW THEY WON."

Don't be ashamed to celebrate every single victory in your life. It doesn't matter how small it is.

Always strive to be a little better every day. Write one more paragraph. Read one more page. Do an extra rep at the gym. Do another phone call at work.

All these actions will compound over time.

126-"If You Wouldn't Settle for You, Why Should Someone Else?"

Are you really living up to all your potential? Are you being the best version of yourself? Would you spend the rest of your life with someone like yourself?

If not, stop trying to find a relationship now and start a deep one with yourself.

Stop chasing the butterflies and begin to work in your garden.

127-"If you're happy and you know it, no one cares."

People don't need to know about every cool place that you go.

You don't need to post every single overpriced or healthy dish you have.

Buying the newest iPhone doesn't mean you are doing well financially.

Stop being an over-sharing attention-seeker. It reeks of desperation for approval.

128-"Don't lose your mind trying to understand someone else's mind."

You can't change what goes through someone else's mind.

Whatever opinion someone has about you, it's none of your business.

Focus on your mental health and be the best version of yourself.

129-"Never stop being a good person because of bad people."

I know mommy and daddy didn't love you enough. Your first girlfriend/boyfriend broke your heart. You got back-stabbed by your best friend. It is 3 am, and your asshole neighbor is having a party with loud music. An idiot parked in the spot that you been waiting for.

Some people suck. Actually, most people suck. However, don't let that change who you are.

By being the awesome person that you were born to be, you will attract into your life people that suck less.

130-"SUCCESS IS THE ONLY REVENGE THAT MATTERS."

All the ups and downs, betrayals, and setbacks don't matter if you win the war. They just help to make your autobiography epic.

Don't waste your time planning negative plots against the ones that did you dirty. Work on improving yourself day and night, and be obsessed with achieving success.

The bullying that you suffered in high school doesn't matter if you earn more than the ones who bullied you. That job you got fired from will not matter once you get a better job. The business you had to close down will be just a distant memory as soon as you open another one. You will not even remember that hottie who rejected you when you have your family with a fantastic partner.

Prove all of them wrong.

131-"Hating popular things doesn't make you a cool person."

Trying to look cool by hating and bitching about things is a great way to keep people away from you.

It usually backfires in your face. You will attract more bees with honey than vinegar.

132-"GET MONEY FIRST, FALL IN LOVE LATER."

You will have plenty of time to meet that amazing person that will break your heart, fuck up your mental health, and leave you financially ruined later in your life.

So, educate yourself and put in the hours, the work, and the effort to become financially secure.

If you ever catch your lovely partner in bed with your best friend, you will recover faster if you cry inside your Mercedes or in first class on your way to Europe.

133-"Karma has no menu. You get served what you deserve."

If you are not an asshole, you don't need to fear Karma. Karma is your best friend because it's the only insurance you have that one day, those special assholes that cross your path will pay for all the dirt that they have done to you.

134-"YOU DON'T HAVE TO REACT TO EVERYTHING YOU COME ACROSS."

You have no idea how much drama you could avoid in your life by keeping your mouth shut.

Social media has given people a sense of importance and relevance. However, the constant need to express your opinion about every single thing makes you look entitled and narcissistic.

Besides, most of the things we tend to react to are negative, and reacting to them can drag you into fights that are not yours, arguments, and unnecessary drama.

Don't fall into the trap of provocations or feed your ego into looking right in some situations. Always choose to keep your peace.

Besides, everyone has a camera on their phones nowadays, so avoid having public meltdowns if you don't want to go viral on social media for all the wrong reasons.

135-"TEENAGERS DON'T HAVE SOULS"

If you are a struggling parent trying desperately to connect with your spoiled brat, don't worry. They haven't fully developed a soul just yet.

Their soul usually starts to develop after their heart gets broken for the first time.

If they are not in love with anybody yet, remember, life is a bitch, and they will know soon enough.

136-"DON'T SHAME YOURSELF INTO CHANGE. INSTEAD, MOTIVATE YOURSELF TO BECOME YOUR BEST VERSION."

We are all faulty beings. Don't ever fat shame, or slut shame, or shame yourself for anything. Your internal dialogue is the most important dialogue that you will ever have. It runs through your mind constantly.

Pay attention to everything that you are mentally consuming. The people that you talk to. What you watch on TV, the books you read, and the information that shows up in your social media feed.

Be kind to yourself, choose to be around positivity, and consume products that motivate you.

137-"STOP TREATING YOUR TRUE PURPOSE IN LIFE LIKE A HOBBY."

S top working 8 hours a day, 5 five days a week, on someone else's dream.

Spend time turning whatever you love and are good at into your full-time job.

Always remember there are girls out there becoming millionaires by selling their farts in jars online.

138-"Make sure your life story is not a cautionary tale for others."

Remember, everybody has a camera on their phones.

So, don't get into fights in public, and don't ask to talk with the managers in restaurants; you don't want to become the next Karen on the internet.

And most importantly, if you ever send a nude photo to someone, don't put your face on it.

139-"If You Never Believe in Yourself, You'll Never Let Yourself Down."

Perfection is a utopia.

Stop pressuring yourself to be perfect. That paralyzes you from reaching your goals.

Recognizing that you are imperfect and will eventually fail in many situations can take away the pressure and motivate you to keep moving.

140-"If someone is too busy to make time for you, maybe you are not a priority."

If there is a will, there is a way.

There is no such thing as a bad time, weekend, or holiday. If someone really wants to stay in your life, they will find a way to. If someone wants you in their lives, they will make room.

Stop treating like "priority" the people who just see you as an "option."

141-"It doesn't matter if you lose the battle if you win the war." -Pyrrhus of Epirus – 279 BC.

All the cold, lonely nights. All the humiliating jobs, with the toxic coworkers. All the times you got back-stabbed by one of your best friends. All the times that your heart got broken and stomped on by someone who you thought was the one.

All the dirt they did to you will not matter if you have the last laugh. If you get the job, if you survive school, if you build the business, if you have your own family.

So, don't feel down if you have to go to bed tonight licking your wounds or if you fall asleep crying. You survived today to fight another battle tomorrow. All the pain and suffering that you are going through will not matter if you win the war.

Success is the only revenge.

142-"Don't judge people's choices if you can't understand their reasons."

We have all have been there. Desperate, drunk, high, broke, lonely, horny. So, don't be so judgmental and self-righteous.

143-"Shit Happens When You Trust in Fake People."

A friendship with a fake person will always end up in the worst way possible; they don't care about you and are just there for what they can gain.

Life is too short to waste time with fake people.

Real friends will never let you down. They are your ride-or-die.

They will defend you even if you are wrong in a situation; then they will tell you how much of a piece of shit you are in private.

144-"Start each day with a goal, so you have something to fuck up."

Plan your day the night before. Make sure to start your day with a plan to move you closer to your goal.

Write it down, choose the clothes you will wear, make your gym bag, prepare your meal.

It doesn't matter how simple your daily target is. Having a purpose helps you leave the bed and focus on something productive.

145-"Fail all the way to your success."

Don't be afraid to fail. Fail more and fail hard.

Being fired from a job can be your opportunity to become an entrepreneur, write a book, start a business, or focus on something you love. Being turned down for a promotion can be a chance to learn new skills and find a job that makes you happy.

A breakup is your first step to meeting your soulmate, or at least someone less trashy than your ex.

146-"You only get to know someone when you say no to them."

Everyone is nice when you are agreeing with them. When you show up for the stupid parties, loan money to them, give the rides, pay for the round of drinks, laugh at the unfunny jokes, and share the check equally even though you only had the small salad.

Say no, and people will start showing their true colors.

Start to say no and watch your circle of friends get smaller.

147-"The only thing worse than mornings are "morning people."

D on't be one of those; only engage in conversations or interactions with people once they have their morning coffee.

148-"NEVER TELL YOUR PROBLEMS TO ANYONE. 20% DON'T CARE, AND THE OTHER 80% ARE GLAD YOU HAVE THEM."

Most people are fighting their own battles. They are just too busy trying to survive to live another day. So, as much as they seem to care about your problems, they simply can't do it sincerely.

On the other hand, some people are actually happy when something goes wrong in your life. Some even appear to be rooting for your success, but underneath, they can't wait to see you fail.

So, don't expect anything from anybody, and keep your problems and victories to yourself.

149-"Silence is the best reply to a dickhead."

There is nothing worse for a narcissistic person than indifference.

A narcissist feeds on causing drama and contention. Once you don't react, they lose their powers.

Don't feed the trolls, and they will starve to death.

150-"WHEN WORK FEELS OVERWHELMING, REMEMBER THAT YOU'RE GOING TO DIE."

Remember, you are not coming out of life alive. There is a liberating feeling of acceptance. Instead of wasting all your time and energy on anxiety and fighting to fix things that can't be fixed, embrace the worst-case scenario.

Yes, you will get fired. Yes, the exam results came back positive. Yes, your partner is cheating on you. Yes, and now what? The worst came to worst. Push came to shove.

You must find the strength to pick up all the pieces and move on. The only way out is through. Keep moving, and eventually, you will get out of the situation as you have done many times before.

151-"To become a diamond, a stone has to survive the pressure."

Diamonds are some of the most expensive stones out there, and for a stone to become a diamond, it has to endure through high pressure and extreme temperature.

Like diamonds, champions are not born champions; they are made. Nobody becomes a great athlete, writer, artist, or professional in any field by only existing.

Embrace the process, the early mornings, the late nights, the extra hours in the field, the loneliness, the injuries, the pain, the suffering, and the joy.

Learn to love the process, and once you have survived, you will become a much better person, and the victory will taste even more sweet.

152-"IF YOU ARE IN HELL, HUG THE DEVIL."

Now and again, we fall into the trap of entitlement and victimhood. That can mask the situation, as people will feel sorry for you and give you the fake illusion that if it is not fair, you shouldn't probably have to go through this situation.

However, as you probably have realized by now, life is unfair. Stop crying and playing the victim.

Accept the situation and embrace the madness. Make peace with your destiny by respecting the process, and keep moving.

153-"Stop pretending you know everything. You are not Google."

Nowadays, knowledge is at the tip of our fingers. We can get answers with a few clicks or just by asking the question out loud. So, being a "smartass" with a solution or opinion for every question or subject people throw at you isn't a sign of wisdom.

People can actually start to perceive you as obnoxious or narcissistic. Things can get even worse if you do not know what you are talking about. A simple internet search can diminish your credibility and open the opportunity for people to call you out on your bullshit.

So, fight the urge to always have an opinion about everything. Be a good listener, and learn about other people's world views.

154-"SOME RED FLAGS COME SHAPED LIKE A HEART."

Don't trust your feelings about someone you just met. Mostly, don't trust your feelings for someone who gave you the best sex you had in months.

Relationships and trust are built over time.

Take your time getting to know the other person and acknowledging all the red flags instead of waiting to know how many shades of red a flag can have.

154- "If haters are going to hate! Make sure they hate you even more!"

It doesn't matter how nice you try to be with people that don't like you. They will hate you, bitch about you, and betray you at their first opportunity.

Even Jesus knew that when he said: "Don't cast pearls to the pigs!"

So, stop wasting your time with people who don't care about you or don't even like you. Cut them out of your life, and for those that have to stay, make sure they know better that fuck with you.

156-"Sometimes the One Thing That You Want the Most Is the Best Thing That Never Happens to You."

D on't cry over the things that didn't work out. There is always something better on the horizon.

The promotion you didn't get can be the first step to getting a better job elsewhere or starting your own business. The ex that broke your heart can lead you to meet the love of your life.

It was never meant to be. Don't waste your time crying over the past.

Rejection means redirection.

157-"WE LIVE IN A WORLD WHERE COMPANIES STILL HAVE TO PUT DIRECTIONS ON SHAMPOO."

There will come a time in everyone's life when we will meet an idiot who makes us understand why companies still have to put these directions on the bottle.

158-"Get ready for more of the same."

Albert Einstein said: "The definition of insanity is doing the same thing over and over and expecting different results."

Your life today is a direct result of your choices from yesterday.

If you keep doing the same things, seeing the same people, going to the same places, and having the same kind of food, you will keep getting the same results.

159-"Sometimes you don't hate someone, you just lose all the respect you have for them."

All circles must come to an end.

When you lose respect for someone, you will never be able to see that person in the same way.

However, this doesn't mean that person has changed or you must become their enemy.

Sometimes, you are the one that has outgrown the relationship; things that were important before don't have the same meaning now.

Not everybody in your life now is meant to be part of your future. Some people must go to make room for exciting and more interesting people in life.

160-"Don't Waste Your Time with Meaningless Friendship, Forced Interactions, or Unnecessary Conversations."

We have all gone through at least five wars, way too many economic recessions, and a plague that closed down the whole world. All of this served to show how fragile we are and how time is our most valuable resource.

Don't waste your life and precious time conforming to social norms by keeping relationships, careers, jobs, positions, or anything that doesn't make you happy.

161-"LIFE IS MOSTLY JUST LEARNING HOW TO LOSE."

It doesn't matter how hard you try; you will never be able to control the outcomes in your life. You can train, learn, prepare for it, and endure, but you will never be able to predict fate.

The only real thing we can control is our mindset and, therefore, how we react to the adversities that life throws at us. We can choose to find love again after a breakup or close ourselves off to people. Finding a better job, starting our own business after losing a job, or dwelling on resentment for being fired.

Accept failure as a redirection into a better path to achieve your dreams and keep moving.

162-"YOU DON'T HAVE TO FIGHT FOR A SPOT IN SOMEONE'S LIFE IF THEY WANT YOU TO BE THERE."

S top ignoring red flags.

If someone wants to see you, they will make it happen. If someone wants to talk with you, they will call.

But if someone calls you at 3 am after two weeks of silence, you're just a booty call.

163-"Everyone's Entitled to Their Very Stupid Opinion."

We still live in a free society. Being stupid isn't illegal yet.

So, take a deep breath and just smile at their ignorance.

164-"Always strive to be less of a piece of shit than you were yesterday."

Comparing yourself with others is a recipe for failure and low self-esteem.

The only person that you supposed to be comparing yourself to it, is the person that you were yesterday.

We usually underestimate the power of the compounding effect. However, the little actions that we take every day towards our goals can amount to great results.

165-"It is what it is. And it's not good."

Realizing that everything is fucked, takes away the power of anxiety.

Imaging the worst-case scenery came to fruition. You got fired. You didn't get the girl. He cheated on you with your best friend. You are broke. The test is positive. Now what? There is no time to be desperate. The worst has already happened.

Don't indulge in self-pity or ruminate about how things should have been. Acknowledging how bad things are is the first step to getting back into the right track.

166-"DON'T EXPECT PEOPLE TO STICK AROUND IF YOU WOULD BREAK UP WITH YOURSELF IF YOU COULD."

Take a really good look at yourself.

Do you really think that you deserve a second chance in your relationship?

If you can't stand yourself, why should someone else?

The only relationship you should be working on is within yourself.

167-"BROKEN CRAYONS STILL COLOR."

Give people a chance.

So, what if she has already been married four times? Or if he just got out of prison.

168-"STOP LETTING BLIND PEOPLE TELL YOU WHAT TO SEE."

Don't accept financial advice from people who are broke. Don't take relationship advice from someone who is on their third wedding, and stop taking life advice from alcoholic depressed people.

169-"Live Each Day As If It's Your Last And Someday It Will Be."

The idea that we only live once, it's a lie perpetuated by today's society that celebrates a vapid lifestyle.

We live every day and only die once.

There is nothing wrong in enjoying a glass of wine or a beer at the end of a long day of work, or having your favorite caloric food every now and again, or even partying on the weekend. The problem is when we start to over indulge in those things.

170-"There are 3 am friends and 6 pm friends. Learn how to differentiate them."

In an ideal world, your friends would be there for you no matter what.

However, we are talking about real life, and you probably already notice that there are different kinds of friends.

There are friends you can ask for help, who you can cry with, and who you can be yourself without using a mask.

On the other hand, there are some friends who you can count on only when you get paid or want to go out, get drunk, gossip about other people, and do fun stuff in general. There is nothing wrong with those friends. They are great. However, learn the difference and always prioritize the real ones.

171-"Pain is inevitable and unavoidable."

There are three certainties in life: death, taxes, and pain. The sooner you accept that pain is part of the process to success, the easier your path to making your dreams come true will become.

Stop waiting until things get better or less painful to fight for your dreams.

Acknowledge the pain, and keep moving ahead.

172-"CHOOSE A GOOD HEART OVER A GOOD FACE."

Everyone likes to complain about the higher divorce rates in to-day's world. Nobody talks about whether these people should be together to begin with.

We live in a society that celebrates beauty and youth. We praise faces and bodies. Meanwhile, intelligence and values take a backseat to our judgment.

That doesn't mean good-looking people lack those qualities or that ugly people have them. However, when it comes to our relationships, instead of prioritizing looks, we should also take into consideration factors like integrity, morals, ethics, culture, decency, common sense, and a clean criminal record.

So, next time you meet someone new, make sure that a hot body also comes with a good heart.

173-"Your Life Today Is A Reflection Of Choices Of Yesterday."

Never underestimate the power of the compound effect. The little actions that you take today will pay big dividends in the future. Whatever you are going through now are directly results from your actions a year ago.

So, choose wisely. Order the salad instead of the cheeseburger. Don't skip the workout because it is raining. Read the book instead of binge-watching Netflix for hours.

Doing the hard stuff now will make things easier in the long run.

174- "Disappointed but not surprised."

Never underestimate the power of positivity in your life. However, know the difference between being positive and being naïve.

Always wait for the best, but prepare for the worst.

It helps to ease the pain of disappointment if you already expect that knife in your back.

175-"Happiness is just lack of information."

Would you quit your job and start your own business if you knew that 90% of new businesses fail in the first year? Would you have a child if you calculated all the amount of money that you would need to provide until the kid turns 18? Or if you know how little you will get to sleep from the day that baby is born.

How often do we stop going after something we really want because we are overthinking and overanalyzing?

We feel the need to know and plan everything. Our brains are not designed to make us take risks. It's designed to keep us safe; it always seeks comfort. It's able to give you an infinite number of reasons not to go work out, not to ask that special person out, not to start a new business or relationship.

So, stop overthinking and overanalyzing before you make every single decision in your life. It leads to inertia. Go for it; just do it.

176-"DON'T KILL THEM WITH KINDNESS. PUNISH THEM WITH YOUR HAPPINESS."

Nothing will hurt your haters more than seeing you achieving your goals and dreams.

It's not worth fighting, arguing, or being nice to your haters.

The best revenge against them is your success.

177-"Sucking is the first step to being great a something."

If a baby stopped trying to walk because he fell on his first attempt, he would never walk. The same would happen if a child gives up learning how to ride a bike after one try.

A recipe for failure is to try to be perfect. Perfection is just an illusion.

You will never be good at something in your first attempt. You most likely will suck, but then you will suck less, and eventually, if you don't give up, you will get good at it.

178-"If you always have to be the bigger person, stop hanging around little people."

We all have our bad days and are capable of being insensitive to the people around us sometimes. However, if you constantly need to apologize or walk on eggshells around a friend, it's a sign that this friendship is already dead.

A true friendship provides a safe space to be who you are.

Real friends are able to recognize their mistakes and apologize like mature people instead of blaming others.

179-"Forgive your enemy, but remember the bastard's name."

Remember to always save all "screengrabs" and voicemails in a special folder on your phone.

Nowadays, you never know when your "Best Friend Forever" will backstab you.

180-"THE WORSE KEPT SECRET IN THE WORLD IS: NO ONE ACTUALLY KNOWS WHAT THE FUCK THEY ARE DOING."

Don't be fooled by appearances. People only pretend they know what they are doing with their lives.

They try to hide behind their PhDs, business plans, and social media posts.

However, we are all the same—85% water and 15% anxiety.

181-"Forgiveness doesn't equal 'forgetness'!"

Forgive, forgive, and forgive.

There are actually scientific studies about the power of forgiving someone. It can bring you peace and closure. It makes it easier to continue on your path to success if you don't have to carry the burden and the load of holding a grudge.

That being said, forgive, but don't ever forget what the bastard did to you.

Forgiving an ex after they cheated doesn't mean you should get back with them. Forgiving someone who borrowed money from you and never paid doesn't mean you should lend them more money. Forgiving a friend who was gossiping about you doesn't mean you should tell them all your secrets again.

182-"It's better to fail in originality than succeed in imitation." – Herman Melville

Stop being just another follower. Stop being influenced by influencers.

In a day and age where everyone seems to be in a competition to be average by dressing in the same clothes, eating the same food, going to the same places, and listening to the same music, embrace your uniqueness in all your glorious weirdness.

183-"Change that "one day" to "day one.""

There is never a right time to start chasing your dreams.

You are never too old because today is the youngest that you have ever been in your life.

184-"STRESS IS USUALLY CAUSED BY GIVING A FUCK."

Sometimes, all the stress, anxiety, and overthinking are just a waste of time. You should always grab the wheels of destiny and forge your own path through life.

However, some situations are out of your control, and you must accept this. The good news is that you would be surprised by how many bad situations will sort themselves out if you just don't give a fuck.

Some things have to come to an end in order to make space for better things.

Crack open that beer, put your feet up, and catch up on that latest episode of your favorite series. Let things fall into place. Trust the process.

185-"It's better to have an honest asshole by your side than a likable liar."

It's better to be stung by the truth than be slowly poisoned by lies.

A real friend will be by your side in the tough times, but will not think twice to call you on your bullshit.

186-"Living life in the hardest way makes it easier."

Working out and eating healthy is hard. Starting your own business is hard. Going back to school or learning a new skill is hard. Saving money, setting boundaries in your relationship, and going the extra mile at work is also hard.

However, being out of shape and sick is also hard.
Staying for years at the same deadening job is also hard.
Being broke and alone is also hard.
Being stuck in an unhappy relationship is also hard.

Choose your hard wisely.

187-"Never do anything you wouldn't want to explain to the paramedics."

The answer is always NO when your friend wants you to try an exotic drug that you never heard about.

Or when your partner wants you to try a sexual toy that is bigger than 8 inches.

188-"People are really great as long as you don't get to know them."

Never trust anyone right away.

Trust and real friendship are built with time.

It doesn't matter how funny, nice, or friendly they appear to be. People suck.

Ellen DeGeneres exists to prove that.

189-"LIFE IS A BITCH, BECAUSE IF IT WAS A SLUT, IT WOULD BE TOO EASY."

If life were easy, we would all be millionaires, living on mansions, popping champagne for breakfast. However, nobody appreciates things that come too easily.

Life has a twisted way of testing you, breaking you, and ultimately transforming you into a better person.

Embrace the process, journey, the pain, the setbacks, the closed doors, the lessons that you learn along the way.

Because your victories will taste even sweeter if you know you earned them.

190-"The best motivation to fall in love quickly is to split rent."

This applies especially to cities with high rent prices, such as London, New York, Sao Paulo, and Los Angeles.

The best reason to take the next step in a relationship is when you are unsure about it. It's saving money on rent.

Why pay for individual rent, plus expensive dinners and motel rooms, if you guys can order pizza and have sex on your living room floor in between episodes of your favorite Netflix series?

If the relationship ends, you can always look back and smile at how much money you saved.

191-"When You Think You Can't Live Without Love, Remember Oxygen Is More Important."

Nobody has ever died of a broken heart.

It will hurt, but you will survive that cheating bastard.

192-"DON'T FOCUS ON THE MOUSETRAP. FOCUS ON THE CHEESE AND THE CHALLENGE."

Keep your eyes on the prize.

Be positive, and always see the cup as half full.

There are people getting rich right now by selling photos of their feet and jars with their farts.

193-"As soon as they stop talking to you, they will start talking about you."

Don't ever tell your secrets to anybody. It doesn't matter how nice you think they are.

Every backstabber was once someone's BFF.

194-"Don't let that cheat meal become a cheat lifestyle."

Time goes by fast; one day, you are having a cheat meal, and suddenly, it's three years later, you are 156 pounds heavier.

Don't ever underestimate the power of the compound effect, the results of the little actions you take daily. For better and for worse.

The healthy meal choice and workout you don't skip can be the difference between a heart attack and a fit body. The money you save instead of getting the newest iPhone can make the difference between having money for an emergency or getting yourself in debt.

Be wise about all your choices; it doesn't matter how small or mundane.

195-"Doing your best doesn't mean working yourself to a mental breakdown."

S top working to make someone else's dream come true.

Prioritize your dreams, your family, your physical and mental health.

196-"Don't hate someone for what they look on the outside. Hate them for what a piece of shit they are on the inside."

B eing an adult is realizing the difference between a demanding boss and an asshole that needs to be reported to the HR department.

The difference between a hard-working dad and an a dad going to a midlife crisis.

The difference between an overprotective mother and real-life Faye Dunaway in Mommie Dearest.

197-"Reset, refocus, readjust, restart, and stop giving a fuck."

Whatever path you decide to follow in your life, it will be much better if you stop caring about what other people think.

198-"BE CAREFUL HOW FAR YOU PUSH SOMEONE AWAY. THEY MAY END UP LIKING IT THERE."

D on't push someone away and expect them to be there for you when you're ready.

199-"THEY'D MAKE TIME FOR YOU IF THEY WANTED TO."

Sometimes, the truth is hard to swallow. Maybe he's just not that into you. Maybe you are not her type. Maybe you were just a one-night stand thing. Get over it and move on.

200-"Whatever you are, be a good one."

Embrace your weirdness and uniqueness.

Be the nicest person in your circle of friends or the biggest asshole.

Go all in. Be bold and unapologetic. Loud and proud.

Embrace the pain, the tears, and the joy of being who you are.